My Exit Interview:

A Remedy For Quiet Quitting

By Jim Weaver

RoseDog Books
PITTSBURGH, PENNSYLVANIA 15238

RoseDog Books
585 Alpha Drive, Suite 103
Pittsburgh, PA 15238
Visit our website at *www.rosedogbookstore.com*

ISBN: 979-8-88812-401-7
eISBN: 979-8-88812-901-2

Table of Contents

*To all those sales representatives
that had a manager ride in their passenger seat
for a few days.*

Earlier in my sales career, I attended a sales training seminar. This was an excellent seminar, and I learned some very helpful information. One of the speakers gave a quote that has stuck with me ever since and is still true today and probably every day moving forward.

"If you always do what you have always done then you will always get what you have always gotten."

This book may open your eyes to a better way.

Prologue

My first sales job was selling shoes in our downtown shoe store over the Christmas break. I was a junior in high school, and this shoe store was small and not high-end at all. A nicer shoe store was down the street, but the location of this store was perfect for foot traffic for holiday shopping.

A gentleman that previously worked for my father, when he had a furniture business downtown, had moved on and was now manager at this retail shoe store. He was a great guy and quite fond of our family. He called the house one evening and spoke with my dad, and then dad called me to get on the phone. "Johnny would like to speak with you," he said. I grabbed the phone. "Hello?" He offered me a job for the holidays.

I had never sold shoes, or for that matter, never sold anything. He assured me I would do well and that all that was needed was some good training and a good work ethic.

"Okay, and how do I get these?"

He said, "Let's start next week."

"I do not get out of school for another two weeks."

"I know, but the key to selling is training, trust, and a good work ethic. You develop these and everything else sort of falls into place. Come in from 6 pm to 8 pm every day next week and I will train you. Plus, I will pay you."

I came in and shadowed him from 6 pm to 7 pm, the last hour of business. The door closed at 7 pm and business was over for the day. I learned a lot from watching and listening. The next hour, from 7 to 8 pm, was him providing detailed training and offering suggestions. He then helped me learn that enthusiasm is the main ingredient in work ethic. Customers will drop their defenses once they see how much you care about their needs. This is true with everything, but for now—it's shoes, and I had a lot more to learn. Each day I learned more and more. At the end of the week, I knew my stuff. He knew that I knew it, too. "Hey," he said, "I know you don't start for another two weeks, but if you would like to earn some extra spending cash I could use some help this weekend."

Sure I could use some extra money. I came in on Saturday and worked and continued working during the week if school or basketball did not interfere. I was starting to learn the art of closing the deal. The more I watched him, the more I learned. His sales process was shorter and his total value per sale was higher than mine. Not only was I taking longer to close the deal, but my deals were worth less. What was I doing wrong?

Aw, yes, a big fault of most salespeople is not knowing when the customer is ready to buy. This training comes with experience. You must first learn how to sell, then go out and sell. The sales process is like an engine. It requires tune-ups to perform better. Adjustments here and there will make the engine run better. He then said, "Listen for buying signals." He also taught me to make a few closing comments myself. Work on getting them to say yes as soon as possible. Once you do, then get them to the cash register as soon as possible. Why do you think we have all these ancillary items at the register? These are the additions that create extra value for your order. When the customer is excited about their purchase, this is the perfect time for add-ons. The worst-case scenario is you just sell them some shoes. This is true with all sales. When they are ready to close and sign, that is a perfect opportunity to gain a little more.

That was fifty-two years ago and it is still true today. I continued with summer and winter jobs until I graduated from college. After a fun summer job with college buddies, we all went our separate ways and started our working careers. My first real sales job came in 1983. Over the next forty years, I had the opportunity to work in sales and sales management for some outstanding companies. I also worked with a few startup companies that were great ideas at the time, but circumstances changed that. My accomplishments remind me of a decorated war hero. I won every award you can win in the game of sales. I also have had every type of manager you can come across.

I have been managed by every management style in existence. I have also been able to watch them perform as well as those above them. I believe there is a better way. Because of COVID, the sales process has been changing. No one had a clue we were having a problem under the pre-COVID sales process. We just did not know what we did not know. Now, I see the sales process evolving into a platform that has everyone on the sales team operating more efficiently and at a much lower operational cost. Change is inevitable. Those that embrace change and learn to master the new paradigm will be quite successful.

Earlier this year, my current employer was acquired by a much larger corporation. Last week the new owner laid off a large number of legacy employees, and I was one of them. This book is not only a message for the president of the company but speaks for the sales representatives of many other companies. Who ever gets an exit interview with the president? Exactly. Maybe a handful of sales representatives have had exit interviews/conversations with the president. Since it rarely occurs, I decided to write about what it may be like. Thus, this is my exit interview with the president. I just wanted to bring my thoughts to your attention. I would imagine that most field sales organizations, as well as other employees throughout the world, share my thoughts. I think every employee leaving a company, no matter the reason, should have an exit interview. It's a no-brainer to me! Just think about the information made available to the company. How cool would it be to speak with the president in this type of interview? In my opinion, CEOs, directors, and presidents of companies would learn so much by regularly meeting directly with the sales force: get the answers to questions or hear comments firsthand. No cover-up at all. The message would be coming directly from the frontline.

I know in many companies, human resources have an exit interview strategy in place for individuals leaving the company. This process usually involves the employee speaking with human resources or a director (some level of management above their current manager). This is a corporate feel-good tool. They pat themselves on the back for creating this exit strategy. Has anything come from these interviews? Has any corporate policy changed? I would imagine most information gathered from these interviews was filed in the cylinder cans beside the desk…

Before COVID, company presidents received sales information from field reports as well as from those reporting to the president. There is a possibility that the interpretation of the field sales reports was shaded by blame focused on the inability of the sales force. Everyone in corporate America has become very good at pointing the finger. But the blame lies elsewhere. It is easy to blame field sales because they are not there to defend themselves and neither are their managers. It is usually directors and higher-ups in these executive meetings, so the blame is easily pushed downhill. The message the directors take with them departing the meetings is, "Train them more, work them harder, ride with them more, put them on a plan, and cut their pay." These are the regular culprits that would show up when the quota was not hit. A common default mode in sales management is 'management by intimidation.' Push them harder and sales should improve. Maybe, but is there a means that is beneficial to the entire team?

Since there has been a paradigm shift occurring, I felt I needed to deliver a message directly to the president. I believe this book encompasses everything that would be said in a conference room containing field sales representatives and company presidents. The goal is to educate you about the issues and offer a guide to work you through this massive paradigm shift. Not only will this book set you up to be a successful salesperson post-COVID, but it will create a work environment that operates with efficiencies at all levels and lower costs. Everyone must know the customer, but not by the means we have been using. The sales representative has been charged with organizing all meetings. Everyone needs to know the customer and there should be no reason why they can't organize their customer encounters. A divide-and-conquer approach may offer more rewards.

I mentioned that I was laid off from my job in late 2022. I have worked for this company for six years and have been quite successful with a recent promotion to Senior Territory Manager. A large medical device company acquired us months earlier, and last week, they laid off a large number of legacy employees. During the conference call that we were all invited to the evening before, they kept reassuring us this was not about performance but mainly due to geographical location. For this big medical device company to be solvent and protect its future, this was a necessary move, and unfortunately, we were the victims. I was okay with this because I had seen it before. However, something hit me this time. I was getting a chuckle out of the whole situation. I found a lot of humor in their desire to spin a message created by a bunch of consultants hired to guide them through the acquisition.

I never knew that the people laid off last week were pivotal as to whether this multibillion-dollar company was going to make it or not. We stay they go under. We leave and the future is good. Is the future good? How many years of experience left the company that day? Will the customer relationships and trust remain the same? How do the other employees now feel? Will they be leaving soon? There will be costs for decisions made, but if your pockets are deep enough, then time will correct the situation and eventually balance things out. This is the norm for business acquisitions in the 21st century! I am at a stage in my life where actions like this are less impactful on my overall well-being. This time I am almost thankful for their decision to let me go. This gave me the time needed to share my thoughts.

I now have the opportunity to write this book. I wanted to get my point of view out to the public. I know many share my same sentiments but have no way for their voice to be heard. Well, I have a bit of time on my hands, so I plan to deliver the message. I believe I speak for others, but if it's just my opinion, then that's fine too. I am glad I am taking the time to put it to paper.

Is the president in the conference room yet? Yes. Let's begin the exit interview. You have approximately one hour to meet. Near the end of this period, I will knock on the door, so you two can finish up the discussion. Knock knock. "Come in."

Chapter 1:

What I Am Not Here To Discuss

"Thank you so much for agreeing to meet with me and hear my thoughts. This hour is very precious to me, so if you don't mind, I would like to lead this meeting. I have so much that I would like to share with you, and fitting it into one hour is going to be challenging. I hope you will have questions, but fielding those during this meeting will not allow enough time for me to express my thoughts. Therefore, I will follow up on this meeting in writing, and if you have questions, I will be happy to address them then.

I am not here to discuss the core ideology and vision you have in place. Nor am I interested in the mission, values, and guiding principles. That is way above my pay grade and something you and your team should embrace. What you create will be your envisioned future. It will be what everyone working for you aspires to be. If you take a little time to travel back to the '80s, you can read about numerous companies creating mission statements. There was an acronym created for what companies were doing to align everyone. The acronym MVGP (mission, values, and guiding principles) was the first step to synchronizing all departments. Next, the companies' business objectives, strategies, and tactics became aligned and consistent with the MVGP. This is still true today and just as important now as back then.

I am not here to discuss hiring practices because I know so little about that process. I do know a lot about the result. It's critical to get the right person for the job. It's that simple. Make sure you have the right people on the team. Society is going to make this task extremely difficult for you, but I suggest not wavering. Place the right people in the job! They will need coaching and training and will be polished to shine with success if they are the right person for the job.

I am not here to tell you how to do your job, but before I start with what I would like to say, I have a question. How is the company able to keep its MVGP and be highly visionary? Have you seen changes since these values were conceived? Please do not answer the question now. Just think about it during our discussion today and throughout the week. I know you could answer it now, but hopefully, this meeting will make you rethink a few things. Let's begin."

Chapter 2:

The New Hire

I have had a dozen different jobs so far in my career. I believe I know a little bit about being a newly hired employee on the sales team. I say 'team' because I held multiple positions on the sales ladder. Of course, I have been a sales representative, but also a sales manager and a sales director. After a few attempts in sales management, I knew that was not for me. I might not know what I want in life, but I quickly figured out management was not for me. At least the way I was taught to manage.

You probably ask, "Why?" It's not that I did not like managing people and helping them be successful; it's the quagmire of corporate inefficiencies that drove me crazy. Plus, if you were not a yes-person, then that was a big strike against you. I knew early on that the system needed to be fixed, but it took an epidemic like COVID for a new and better way to surface.

The system I believe we needed to fix most of the time offered progression and opportunities to those willing to relocate and say yes to everything their managers delivered to them. The first question that should come to mind after reading the last sentence is? Do we have the most qualified and right people in each position? We will not attempt to answer now because your confirmation comes after completing this book.

Back to training. Training is critical to everyone's success. No matter what your position may be, training is required to help you excel. That is especially true in sales, and I mean at all levels of sales. Your sales team is your frontline communicator with the customer, which can make or break you. Therefore they must be polished, poised, and positive. They will need to develop into a trusted advisor to each customer. The customer must enjoy the time spent with salespeople and believe that the return on investment for the time they took was well worth it. If not, you will find meeting times harder to get and not last as long. Once you start to see that, then you know something is not working. The end of the world has not come upon you, but you must be able to understand when your message, and you, have lost value to the customer. Unfortunately, companies today are oblivious to this message. Why? Well, there is a list of reasons why, and we will discuss them throughout the book.

Invest in training. Think about adding to your training budget now. Let's drill down and take a closer look at how I believe training should be moving forward. First, I would like to discuss field sales training. Second, look at next-level management training, and finally, discuss director and executive-level training.

Your sales representatives need to be armed with knowledge about the products as well as training on the sales process your company has adopted. There is no one sales process that works for all. However, everyone in sales must be knowledgeable about the product or process and be trustworthy, likable, dependable, and enthusiastic. You can always come up with more characteristics they should embody, but the ones I mention are essential. They open the customer up to like you and drop their guard. This way, they will be willing to hear your message. If you have a good product, salespeople are trained well enough, and the customer has a need, then you should be able to negotiate an order.

Before the newly hired sales representative comes to training, study material should be sent in advance. This needs to be high-quality material, and they need to spend ample time studying it, so they are knowledgeable about the product or process on day one of training. The intent here is not to cut their time in training by having them perform the home study. No, no, this is to get them well-prepared for the class or on-site training. Do not overload them to the point that they will just rush through and create a system that allows completion without learning. You want them to learn not to drink out of a fire hose. There must be knowledge checks that help the individual understand they are making progress. Your training team, if trained properly, will be able to develop such a curriculum!

Once the new hires arrive for formal training, there should be a knowledge check that lets you know if they are ready to move forward. If some seem more ready than others, then a system needs to be in place to get everyone on equal ground. This is a good marker for everyone. "Is our training process correct?" If not, then make the necessary adjustments. "Did we hire the right people?" After every training class, there should be program evaluations to make sure what you are doing is the best it can be. That is just common sense.

Who should perform the training? This is the broken part of the process. Companies are too quick to outsource this need. They jump at the chance to hire consultants or third parties to conduct the daily training. As a sales training participant, I never understood this decision. Well, let me restate that. I understood it was easier and cost-efficient to do it this way. However, everyone in the class is learning from someone that was trained at school or by reading books. Is your training team made up of individuals that have sold the product or service they are training you for? I doubt it, and why? It costs too much. Okay, I agree it will cost more to have those that excelled in selling your product take on the new role of trainer. To get them into this role, you will have to offer promotions and pay increases to get them onboard.

This is a perfect example of selling. Companies look at this and say it would cost too much, but in sales, we are always overcoming the cost objectives by getting the customer to look at the total cost versus the upfront cost. Are you better off having a book-trained individual that has never spent years in the field selling your product and training your representatives or having a successful sales representative training the team? The successful sales representative can share real-world experiences and discuss strategies and tactics that do and do not work. I believe the newly trained sales representatives will be better equipped for their job and able to provide a better return on the training investment. I haven't read the studies to prove this point, but again, common sense should win here.

There will always be those that rank higher. Some will finish first in the class and some will finish toward the bottom. However, everyone must be proficient enough to represent the company. As for training details, I will leave that to the training team. The participants must learn and be ready for the next phase in their learning process. It makes no sense to train them once and then expect their performance to be flawless. Once they pass the initial on-site training, it is time for phase two.

Send them out in the field to study with others. They should work with field trainers that achieved this status by excelling in their performance. Have a program in place for these individuals to continue the sales training but in more of a real-world scenario. These field trainers are in the positions because of their past performance and desire to advance in the company. Doing it this way establishes a pool of people to draw from for sustaining your in-house corporate training program. The in-house team will advance or possibly leave, so you now have a good replacement pool to choose from. I am a firm believer that employees benefit from moving into new roles. Again, it's just common sense.

When the new hires are in phase-two training, there should be goals and objectives for them. I will leave this up to the training team, but each individual should come out from phase two better equipped than when they arrived. They should be eager to get into the field and start performing. But that would be a big mistake to send them into the field. I believe phase three should be a customer shadow program for at least a day or two.

I spent most of my sales career in the medical device field. Every company I worked for had a physician speaker/consultant team. I believe new hires should go to them for a day or two and shadow them. Of course, this would need to be geographically and cost-efficient, but that's easy enough to coordinate. The new hire should observe didactic presentations given by the physician and then have discussions following these presentations. They should follow the physician wherever they go. Observe their daily routine. This gives them firsthand knowledge of how their customers spend each day. During this shadow time, they should practice their presentations. Get feedback from the physician on their execution and how they could improve. This is the time for them to practice in front of the professionals and then debrief after each attempt. I also believe this could be tweaked to fit into any type of industry.

It is now time to go to work. You are ready to start selling in your territory, and this is phase four of the training process. Get in your office or home office and plan and prepare to meet your customers. Understand who they are, and how they make decisions, and collect as much information as possible. In other words, no need to sell—you are gathering knowledge that will assist you for a long time. I believe you should visit every customer and start the relationship process. With today's technology, this information can be entered into the contact database of choice. The bottom line is you are gathering every bit of information about your customers and their decision-making team. Once you have circulated the territory, then you are ready to start the sales process. This time frame should be a part of the guaranteed payment period. There should be no pressure on the newly hired individual to close a deal. That comes later. One simple tactic that should be expected is to know the special dates for your customers. When is their birthday? Anniversaries, etc.? These should be entered in the calendar with reminders set. Handwritten notes acknowledging such an event go a long way.

It's now time to meet with your manager and put together a sales plan for the next thirty to sixty days. This, too, should be part of the guaranteed payment period. I believe the best plan starts with the representative and is delivered to the manager. This should not be based on a template created by management. That just gives upper management the information they think they need. Have you ever noticed how quarterly business plan templates seemed to change about every quarter to six months? I sure did. That is because they never could settle on what detailed sales information was critical to know and drive the business forward. Therefore, the plan should be created by the new hire and give examples of how they plan to move the business forward and achieve their quota. We will talk about quotas in another chapter.

Over the next thirty to sixty days, there is only so much a new hire can do when it comes to total dollar sales. However, there is a tremendous amount that can be done to drive the relationship forward. This is the critical time for laying the foundation for a great relationship. The new hire should interface with as many individuals on each account's decision-making teams as possible. Their goal should be to gain trust and rapport while introducing the accounts to something to consider buying. Make the presentations and get the decision-makers to consider your proposal. If they see the positive return on investment you are proposing, then there is a good chance they will move forward. Not everyone will. These customers are just as important as the ones that buy.

The final phase, in what I believe to be a great way of preparing new hires to represent your company, is phase five, which requires all newly hired trainees to report back to the home office for a week of training. The first part should be a debrief of phases two through four from a macro view. How did everyone perform as a group in the previous phases? This should then move into a micro view and have each new hire understand how they performed and what areas need improving. Next, the team should discuss their experiences in phase four. What worked, who bought, why did they buy, who did not buy, and why not? Now spend the rest of phase five with the entire group polishing each individual's performance. Utilize the synergy of the group to make everyone better. When the new hires return to their territory, they are off guaranteed payment and start the sales process.

The sales representative is not the only new hire. Everyone benefits from training, but our focus is on the sales team. When it comes to new hires there are managers, directors, key account representatives, marketing, VPs, etc. Anyone directly involved in the sales process needs to be thoroughly trained on the products, programs, and services offered by the parent company. They do not need to go through the five phases of training, but they need to go through phase one and pass. If they are new hires from outside the organization, then I believe they should complete phases one and two in the training process.

Chapter 3:

How I Would Like My Manager to Manage

"I would like to ride with you for three days next week." "I need you to complete this business plan by this date." "Your Monday morning call-in time is…." "Please enter your weekly call points and results." "Please list target accounts." Do these sound familiar? If you are in sales, then you are quite familiar with some variations of the statements above. Rather than the above, let's consider another way.

The ride-with concept is more or less management by intimidation tactic and provides managers with a way to fill their calendars without doing anything. Do not get me wrong—there are times when a ride-with is very important. For instance, when a direct report is new to their job, it makes total sense for the manager to tutor, mentor, and advise. After that, field rides should only come once a year or whenever the representative requests. The annual or semi-annual field ride should be scheduled well in advance, with objectives and strategies clearly defined. This time together allows management an opportunity to evaluate performance and discuss progress year to date.

If the manager is not riding with the representatives, then what on earth are they doing? It is no fault of their own. It's the way the system was designed, and to this design, we started to add layers. As the company and sales grew, so did the layers and, in my opinion, laziness. I think if you sit down and analyze the layers, you may find some inefficiencies. I applaud you if you take the time to study your field sales organizational chart.

Rather than ride with a field sales representative one or two times a quarter, I suggest you help them grow their sales one or two times a quarter. When developing target accounts for each quarter, there should be some for the manager too. A divide-and-conquer approach seems so much more productive to the overall business. If you have the right people in each position, there is no need to check on them quarterly. Help them sell each quarter and everyone benefits. This is not just for first-level managers but should be in place for directors and vice presidents.

The accounts will enjoy having managers, directors, and vice presidents get to know them. You will be in a league of your own for the time being, so reap the rewards. It will not be long before the competition is doing the same. Right now, our business is suffering from a COVID shock. Companies are also experiencing a shock internally. The term for this is "quiet quitting." Just google it and you will be overloaded with definitions. The bottom line is people realized how much they did not like work, or worse, how bad their job made them feel. What I disliked most about most of my sales positions was the manager riding with me. I would have been very excited to have my manager in my territory for three days, calling on key accounts and moving the needle forward. I would be doing the same in another part of the territory. The director and vice president are also doing the same. Now, the territories are buzzing with activities. How nice would it be for the sales process to evolve into a team approach and for the sales team to get to understand the territory and business?

Do we need all the conference calls and meetings we are currently having? Under my proposed sales system, there just would not be time. Companies would be forced to think about what calls and meetings are mandatory. Then, the company would be focused on the customer. The focus is on the customer. Doesn't that sound better?

I once tried to get upper management to visit one of my accounts. They were very interested in meeting the team above my manager and me. I asked the account to provide me with three to five dates that would work for them. They did, and I sent the request and dates to upper management. Not a single date worked because of in-house meetings. At first, you think "okay," but let that sink in a minute. Time is up. Our executive management team was too busy meeting with each other to meet with one of our best customers! This prompted me to start thinking about this book. The customer should be the center point of business, and the entire sales team should develop a relationship with them. Marketing too!

I think the spending budgets in the marketing departments need a little change. I suggest we move funds from brochure creation to marketing department field travel. The marketing department needs to get out and see the customers. Not just the customers that are hired consultants or the customers closest to the office. They need to visit groups of customers from every geography in the country. They should work with the manager's targets and come up with accounts they would like to see. They should then schedule, well in advance, times to meet with these customers. The representatives will be happy to have marketing travel with them to see important customers and discuss their needs, as well as share ideas the company is considering and get their feedback. It is healthy for all involved. More importantly, it provides marketers with information about customer needs. They now know what the customer needs, rather than creating a brochure for the representative to tell the customer what they need.

Now, the sales and marketing teams are working in unison and building customer rapport. They are then able to come back and say, "We heard what you were saying and now have this product, program, or service to fulfill your request." Relationships and trust are being built. At some point in time, you hope to have enough of a relationship that anyone from the corporate office (managers, directors, marketing, and vice presidents) can pick up the phone and call the customers to discuss a topic or need. Business plans need to be built with this focus in mind. The results will follow and probably will cost less.

The business plan has become a worthless tool. At least it has become worthless for the sales representative that is to work the plan. All departments in corporate management have worked their way into the quarterly business plan. The plan template comes from upper management to management, and they then email it to you and say, "Please complete and return by a certain date." Who does this report help? Correct—those that created the template. Now they can run reports or measure progress from their computers. Perfect for them because they can get the information they think they need without leaving their office. The key statement above is information *they think they need.*

I had a wise surgeon I called on that gave me some of the best advice early in my career, at the beginning of our relationship. He said, "There are those people that know what they don't know, and those people that don't know what they don't know!" He then said, "Don't be the latter." The business plan template that comes from corporate down has a lot of "Don't know what you don't know". How could they? They do not know the customer. They may know one or two, but an n of two (n = participants in studies) may not be good for everyone.

The business plan should come from the bottom up and be created from the bottom. If there is clear direction on company goals and sales requirements, then let each create their plan to achieve their objectives. This plan will roll up to the manager to add their information for the accounts to be covered. It then rolls up to the next level and so on. Each individual has a road map to accomplish what they said they would. This now becomes a living document or guide that will be referenced multiple times throughout the quarter. There is no need to do away with a template format, but just make sure each individual can customize it to meet their needs. In addition to this being a business plan, it now also becomes a sales guide.

Who benefits from the Monday phone calls and conference calls? I doubt the customer sees many benefits. A Monday morning call with my manager has been a tactic in almost every company I have worked with.

I guess there is some benefit that comes from these calls, but I really cannot say that it benefitted me. It is a total waste of time. If you have the right people in each job, then there is no need to check up on them every Monday. Stop the calls. The message should be, "If you need me, let me know." "If I need something from you, I will let you know." "If it is that important, then schedule a call or conference call." The standing Monday call-in is being retired.

Why do I need to enter my weekly call points and results? My sales numbers give a very accurate picture of where I am in the process. Entering numbers into a contact management resource (I will not name any, but we all have some sort of a sales database resource we work from) is a waste of time. It is another management intimidation tactic used because of a lack of leadership and creativity. Plus, if everyone in the sales process is customer focused, then they will have a good understanding of what is going on. These databases are good for account information, addresses, and sales history, and many on the sales team may find them quite helpful. However, there needs to be a stop to the tactic of entering the call points, the objectives of the call, and what was accomplished. Do you think what is entered is going to be that helpful?

The target accounts. I have always questioned this request. Especially when we are dealing with such short time frames, like quarters. I will address this later, but quarterly quotas and numbers need to change to annual. We will discuss this later, but how on earth can an account or two make that much difference to territory in a three-month window? It can't, and if it could, then it would probably come at the neglect of the other accounts.

It needs to be understood that a sales representative is responsible for the accounts within their geographical territory. Therefore every account is a target. Individual targets are perfect for managers and above. The representative should sequence their sales process and make the call points geographically efficient. There will be circumstances that change the sequence, but a defined call sequence is a good pathway or guide to follow.

The managers and above need to have target accounts. The ability to determine these targets should be a collaborative effort between the sales representative and the rest of the sales and marketing team. The sales rep and manager should be able to figure out exactly which accounts the manager should call on to help with the sales process. These appointments need to be created by the manager. They should be armed with all account data, so they can schedule their meetings.

The manager will then take his or her target suggestions, as well as the reps' target suggestions, and then send this to the next layer of management. The higher the level of management, the more accounts to deal with, so account priority is required. What accounts offer the best return on investment to the company? Whom do we need to see now? These are very healthy discussions to be had. Under this scenario, we have company personnel out meeting with customers. Sales and marketing are getting firsthand knowledge of customer needs, and they are building great trust and rapport. We need to peel away the layers and get everyone to contribute. It just makes sense to me. Rather than have your employees quietly quit, how about being physically engaged?

Chapter 4:

Filling That Open Position

I know you have mixed feelings about open positions. It is great if the open position is a new expansion position created by company growth. It is not bad when the position is opened because of a promotion. That is a healthy environment allowing the business to operate and develop from within. Positions opened by people leaving the organization are not good, but in a small way, expected. If this is happening a lot, then there is something toxic in the operating system and there is a need for an immediate review.

I believe that great companies are built from within. If you have the right people in place, they share a vision and work toward continuity that protects the core, then you will be successful. Lose any of these key elements and the train may derail. The safest way to protect your company and ensure these elements are preserved is by succession planning at all levels.

Great sports teams have the right players in each position. They also have very good backups in case the starter is out. You are only as good as your weakest link, so make sure all links are strong. You must train and develop everyone to step into the next role when needed. I worry about college basketball today because the great players are one and done. This makes it so hard for the coaches to develop great teams full of backups if needed. The National Collegiate Athletic Association (NCAA) will need to figure out how to address this, and I am sure they will. I am not a basketball coach, but I do like watching the game, so I hope they figure this out. Games are not as much fun to watch nowadays.

Great companies may, at some point, have to deal with a one-and-done scenario, but for now, it is the quiet quitting group that should send a message to the executive team. COVID opened our eyes to this phenomenon, and those that address it quickly will protect the continuity of their companies. Employees at all levels, especially field sales, where I spent most of my time, have become bottlenecked. There is a lack of movement that creates cross-training and development. There needs to be succession training at all levels. If not, you find yourself with a shortage of well-developed successors. Hiring from the outside impedes progress, may cause turmoil, and this hire may end up being a failure. Not to mention what your customers may think. What if they are unhappy?

Having a succession plan to replace everyone keeps the gears synchronized and the engine running well. I recommend that you put a plan in place that carefully prepares everyone for their next role. You want them to take on these new roles because it allows you to build a tremendous talent pool to draw from. It invigorates employees and excites them with new opportunities and upward mobility. You now have taken one of the main reasons why people leave a company out of play. People leave jobs to get better jobs, usually a higher rank with more responsibility and, of course, more pay. If they can have this upward mobility within their own company, then they most likely will not leave. They are proud of their workplace and eager to learn more.

This needs to be done at all levels. Build a training and development program from the bottom to the top. Your team will do what you ask, but if you go and hire from the outside you will lose their commitment, and quiet quitting will be back. However, if you promote from within, you will never have to go for outside talent to get new ideas and talent. Once you put a well-trained employee into a new role, you will see fresh, new ideas and healthy change in the business.

Chapter 5:

Meetings

COVID opened our eyes to in-person meetings. We were all along for the ride. It went without saying, "You must have face-to-face meetings with customers and we need face-to-face meetings within the organization." I agree, but not like how we operated before COVID.

Let's start with the customer. There are plenty of ways to interface with them and maintain the relationship you have in place. If you have been well trained and were considered a value proposition by your customer, then face-to-face meetings are not required regularly. There are so many ways to communicate these days. Learn to be an effective communicator utilizing the latest technology. This allows you to communicate with customers much more efficiently and allows them to interface with you when it is convenient for them. Do not abuse this tactic! Remember, you must maintain a relationship as a trusted advisor. You never want the customer purposely delete your emails, go to voicemail, or turn and walk the other way when they see you.

There is an art to face-to-face meetings. Most companies will teach the two-minute sale; a common name for it is the "elevator pitch." They would like for you to be able to open and close a sales conversation in two minutes or less. It's a great idea, and if the team is trained well enough, then this should come easily to those utilizing the tactic. I found that I had developed strong enough relationships with my customers that I could ask to meet for just a couple of minutes. I knew their schedule for the day in question and would ask to meet after a case, in the hall, at the clinic, end of the day, or before work starts. The customer would usually grant this request and we met. I never abused the process. I came in, delivered my pitch in a few minutes, and then requested follow-up or for them to act on the message at a designated time. They never felt that our encounter was a waste of their time. Your entire team needs to be able to perform this task.

There are also bigger meetings or ones that last longer, like lunch or dinner meetings. You can make a tremendous amount of progress if you utilize these meetings properly. The lunch meeting can be done with only the end user and should be done that way a few times a year. The lunch meeting with the entire office should be done as often as possible. If they are discouraged because of expense, then that thought needs to be reevaluated. The end user of your product, program, or service likes it when you value their entire office. They are part of the process, so they should be included. Plus, you learn so much from relationships with everyone on the account's team.

I recommend scheduling these lunches as far in advance as the customer will go and your company will allow. Take full advantage of both. This will help you build a calendar with a strong foundation of meetings. This is a great opportunity to get extra FaceTime with the customer or customers. They are in good moods most of the time, and the playing field is right to deliver your message(s). Do not be a data dump, throwing everything in the arsenal against the wall looking for something to stick to. Be very strategic with a plan that is well thought out. You will certainly get follow-up meetings or other types of customer encounters from this lunch meeting. Make sure you bring value to every meeting. Is the relationship developing? I am not saying they now want to spend summer vacations with you or go on skiing trips together. Do they enjoy being with you and are there healthy conversations? That is a good goal to shoot for.

By planning these lunch meetings well in advance, you can maintain geographical efficiencies and schedule meetings pre and post with customers that are close by or on the way to and from. Taking the time to proactively schedule is good for your business, minimizes stress, and may afford extra time for your personal life.

Dinner out with the customer. This used to be a common practice and was enjoyed by both parties. The customer dinner has evolved into something that can be done but is not done as regularly as before. Before COVID, the frequency of customer dinners was beginning to slow down. There were rules and regulations on both sides that minimized the number of dinners. Plus, the customer wanted to be with family and friends. Will the customer go to dinner? Yes, but you need to understand what makes them say yes.

The yes-customer. This customer will most likely go to dinner, and all that is needed is to find an open date. When the manager came to ride with you for a few days, this was the customer that usually went to dinner. This is how it would play out.

Manager: "I plan to come to ride with you for three days."

Representatives, thinking to themselves (and this is probably what actually goes through their minds): "Oh man, here we go again. Why is it three days, two days, or one day? Why not come when I need you? Are you just finding a way to fill your calendar? This is wreaking havoc on my work schedule. I need to go to XYZ during the time the manager is going to be here, but that is not important enough for them. They will think I am slack and get on me about that, but actually, those tactics are exactly what I need to do to accomplish my objectives. Oh well, I will forgo that and set up some meetings with the key opinion leaders in my territory and get a few dinners planned. I will keep them busy from early morning until late at night for each day they are here. Not sure what will come from it, but we will be busy with important people."

Does that sound familiar to all you sales representatives out there? I bet so. So what did we get out of the old process mentioned above? We got a disruption in the plan the representative was working on to accomplish their goals. We had to change over to what they thought the boss wanted to see and we needed to keep the boss busy. We then proceeded to spend a large amount of money just so the boss could sit in the passenger seat and have something to do for a few days. Now, there are times this worked well and the ball moved forward. However, most of the time, there was more investment than return. There is time for a change, and I suggest it is now. If the boss would like to be in the field, then please come. I welcome their help with open arms: "Here are the accounts we discussed that would benefit from your involvement; set up meetings and help me, so I can contribute to the overall performance of the region." This is exactly how it should work for them, their boss, and so on up the ladder.

The new product, information, study request, or disruptive technology customer. These are dinners that are super productive and something each company should do as often as possible. To do these numerous times, the company needs to be firing on all cylinders. They need to be producing new products, have compelling new information about existing products, invest in studies to substantiate the significance of their product or have a new disruptive technology that the customer must have to stay competitive. If you have these, then that means your company is reinvesting in itself and building a business platform of growth. Customers would like to be a partner, so they are eager to come to dinner and learn more. There may need to be scheduling, but the customer will work out a time to meet. These are the dinners I would like to invite management to attend. This is the chance to have the team deliver the good news.

Another very important bit of information. Our customers are very busy and work a full day every day. After work is their family time. They are probably struggling to keep a good balance between work and family. Do not push or dilute the credibility you have created. You are a trusted advisor, well-liked, respected, and, at times, part of the decision-making process. Keep that and help it grow stronger. Only request their time when you truly believe it is beneficial to them.

Chapter 6:

Quotas & Compensation

There is a knock on the door. "The meeting will be ending soon."

"Okay, thank you."

"Well, it looks like our allotted meeting time is about to come to a close. Thank you for taking the time to hear my thoughts about changes that might improve the operation of the company."

"Thank you, this has been time well spent and something I now plan to do as much as possible moving forward. Before we end this exit interview, I would like for you to speak with me about quotas and compensation. These seem to be the driving force in sales operations, but so far, you have mentioned nothing about either. Do not get me wrong, everything you have brought to my attention is extremely important, but if you do not mind, please share some thoughts on quotas and compensation. Don't worry about the time. I will handle that. Please proceed."

"Let's start with quotas. I think we all know why quotas have been moved to quarterly versus annual. It is in the best interest of the company and gives them more control over payout. I have heard all the arguments as to why a quarterly system is better, but the reasoning does not add up. I am not here to debate this but rather to explain why I think an annual measurement may be a better indicator of performance. A question to consider. How can you truly understand and measure a sales representative's abilities in a three-month time frame? Another question to consider: do you believe all tactics and strategies put to work in month one of a quarter will come to fruition before the close of month three? I would have to think if you are answering truthfully, then your answer would be, 'no!'

I believe a more accurate measurement of performance is an annual quota. This gives the sales team, notice I mention sales team, the time to put together a great business plan that grows the business to meet and, hopefully, exceed the company's objective. This plan will have everyone on the team, representative, manager, director, VP, marketing, engineering, etc., fine-tuning their involvement with the customer. This cannot be done in a quarter but can be done in a year. I can go on and on, but there is no need because, in my view, the best measurement is annual versus quarterly.

The quota should be an agreed-upon increase of last year's total volume. A very reasonable percent increase over the previous year's volume is what should make up the majority of the quota. You can and should throw in subjective requests to earn more payout and short-term quarterly incentives. These additions can provide the company with an increase in specific sales or measurements needed during the year. It is fun and healthy to request more during the year, but these requests must provide a good return. This simple system will show honesty and character that will be appreciated by the team. The quarterly calculations were like complicated algorithms that always seemed to hide an underlying motive. Take the honest high road with your sales team and they will perform.

Everyone in the company, including you, should be tied into the quota system. Commissions, bonuses, and stock grants should all be based on performance relevant to the quota. This ties everyone together, and the company is a company! I believe you understand my thoughts on quotas. Let's quickly transition into compensation.

The compensation system seems fair to me. I will offer a suggestion that may develop your employees into loyal participants that are less likely to leave the company. Reducing staff turnover is better for everyone and helps you maintain and grow customer relationships. It also provides you with a large pool of talent to choose from in succession planning for your position, as well as every position below yours. My idea is simple.

Make all employees 'stakeholders.' Offer them ways to earn stock. I mean every employee on the payroll. If you offer employees stock, they now feel like a co-owner of the company, and the better the company performs, the more value it brings to them. If they are rewarded with stock, then they are less likely to leave for just an increase in wages. Give everyone performance objectives and if they meet these objectives, then they earn company stock. Each employee should also have the ability to purchase stock at a discount.

If the company does stock buybacks, then this benefits everyone in the company. Buybacks are a common practice, but only the more affluent employees in the company benefit from them. Make it so everyone benefits.

Profits should be shared. As mentioned above, stock buybacks are important and are derived from company profits. Employees should also directly see a monetary benefit from company profits. There should be a system that rewards all employees with a percentage of the profits made that year. This is another excellent means of keeping employee turnover low. Keep the employees happy and performing to the best of their ability. Make them proud to be team members.

Corporate bonuses are nice for C-suite employees, but I believe they should be restructured and become a part of the profit-sharing and quota performance. If the company performs well, then everyone should benefit. Calculating payouts is not my expertise, but you have team members that can easily come up with a fair payout system. The important point is I believe it needs to be done. Everything needs to be tied to company performance and everyone needs to be a participant.

I have delivered my message. That is all I have to say about quotas and compensation. Hopefully, that was helpful. Speaking of help, I hope you got a good return from the time you invested with me. I am a salesperson, so that was my ultimate goal. I will follow up by email and put in writing everything discussed in our meeting today. The attachment will be titled "My Exit Interview." Please review it and if there are any questions or concerns, do not hesitate to reach out to me to clarify. After you have debriefed and had a fair amount of time to think about every-thing, I would like to have a follow-up call. My goal was to deliver a mes-sage that would, hopefully, prompt change. If I succeeded, then I would be more than happy to help with the change. I have some great ideas for the next steps."

Chapter 7:

Email Follow-up

To: (Name), Company President
From: Jim Weaver
Subject: My Exit Interview

(Name),

Once again, thank you for agreeing to host my exit interview. As promised, I have summarized everything discussed in our meeting; please find it attached. If you have any immediate questions, please let me know.

Otherwise, I would like to follow up in a few days to get your feedback. This follow-up will only take a few minutes of your time. I will contact your administrative assistant to schedule a quick call.

Thanks,
Jim

<attached-My Exit-Interview>

To: Jim Weaver
From: (Name), Administrative Assistant to the President
Subject: Follow-up Call

Jim,

Per your request, (Name), President, is available for a follow-up phone conversation on (Date) at (Time). Will this date and time work for you? If yes, please call my direct line (Number) at that time.

Sincerely,
(Name), Administrative Assistant

To: (Name), Administrative Assistant
From: Jim Weaver
Subject: Follow-up Phone Call

That date and time are perfect. I will call your direct line. Make it a great day.

Jim

Chapter 8:

Follow-up Phone Call

"Hello (name of the administrative assistant), is (name of the company president) still available to speak at this time?"

"Yes, sir, I will patch you through right now."

"Thank you very much."

"Hello Jim, I hope you are well?"

"I sure am and I hope you are, too."

"All is good, and thank you for summarizing our meeting last week. It was more than a summary. It was very thorough and covered everything we discussed."

"That is excellent to hear. What are your thoughts? What type of feedback are you able to provide?"

"You have brought up a lot of good points. I agree that the protocol for business commerce is changing. Our meeting and your follow-up helped me understand how important change may be to the success of our company. There were many facets of the business I should be paying more attention to and discussing more with my team. The better questions I ask the better the answers. I will not point fingers and accuse anyone of polishing and cover-up. After our conversation, I am more acutely aware of the importance of a team process to selling. The old approach was the gold standard. It was business as usual. Business as usual has been going on for a long time. You opened my eyes to reevaluating our process. I believe it would be quite healthy to peel back the layers and look again at our mission, values, and guiding principles. A lot has changed since these were developed. It makes great sense to analyze them regularly to make sure we stay the course.

I want to thank you for your thoughts on the sales process. Without our meeting, I would not have given this topic the attention it needed. It is time for a change. The sales protocol needs to be polished, and your team concept is exactly what we were striving to do, but are unable to do. Our system was flawed because we were taking our focus off the customer and we were creating layers to minimize the customer focus. A team with focus is my ultimate goal. I have some ideas on how I plan to move forward with this endeavor, and I plan to execute them immediately. We must act quickly.

You also brought to my attention just how important an exit interview is to the overall well-being of the company. There is so much to learn from an employee leaving the company. Even if there is restructuring or employment was terminated for other reasons, there is important information to be obtained. I also plan from now on to have my executive team and myself involved in exit interviews. We may not be able to attend all exit interviews, but we sure can get some questions answered. I plan to work with human resources to revamp our exit interview policy, so everyone can give parting comments to the executive team of the company. There should be choices for interview formats such as face-to-face, video, phone, or in writing.

I like your belief in training. I concur and like the process, you laid out. I believe more should be added to the process. You opened my eyes to all fingers being pointed at the sales representative. When there was a quota shortfall, the representative usually received all the blame. It's time to move away from this concept. If you have the right people in place, then a team approach should be much stronger than an individual approach. In every team, from time to time, there will be some weaker-than-usual performances. Rather than point the finger at this individual as was done under the old system, take the time to figure out why. Are there disruptive market conditions, personal/family issues, health issues, and on and on? Take the time to understand. Remember, you are only as strong as your weakest link.

If the team member needs additional help or training, then make this available to them. I believe it is time for us to become sales representative advocates rather than blame them for shortfalls.

I also believe it may be very healthy to have an outsider like yourself with a tremendous amount of sales experience communicate with individuals struggling with performance. I could see how these individuals may open up and not be so on guard with their thoughts and conversation. Therefore, if they believe they could benefit from speaking with a sales coach/consultant like you, then I want that available to them. My goal moving forward is to build a great sales team, have all employees as stakeholders, and minimize turnover. Unforced turnover just costs too much, period!"

"Wow, I am overwhelmed. Actually, overwhelmed is the wrong choice of word. I am so excited—that is a better choice. You listened to my exit interview, you read my summary, and now you are putting into action some of my ideas. I have been looking for closure to my sales career, and you have provided what I needed. Thank you for helping me, and I am here to help you in the future if needed.

Thank you so much for speaking with me today on our follow-up call. Make it a great day."

The end!

www.ingramcontent.com/pod-product-compliance
Lightning Source LLC
Chambersburg PA
CBHW051404150726

48000CB00003B/1319